Wait

FIRST POETS SERIES 18

Canada Council
for the Arts

Conseil des Arts
du Canada

ONTARIO ARTS COUNCIL
CONSEIL DES ARTS DE L'ONTARIO

an Ontario government agency
un organisme du gouvernement de l'Ont

Canada

Guernica Editions Inc. acknowledges the support of the Canada Council
for the Arts and the Ontario Arts Council. The Ontario Arts Council
is an agency of the Government of Ontario.

We acknowledge the financial support of the Government of Canada.

Wait

Ned Baeck

**GUERNICA
EDITIONS**

TORONTO – BUFFALO – LANCASTER (U.K.)
2018

Michael Mirolla, general editor
Elana Wolff, editor
Cover and interior design: Errol Richardson
Cover image: Photo by Darlene Fiddler
Guernica Editions Inc.
1569 Heritage Way, Oakville, (ON), Canada L6M 2Z7
2250 Military Road, Tonawanda, N.Y. 14150-6000 U.S.A.
www.guernicaeditions.com

Distributors:
University of Toronto Press Distribution,
5201 Dufferin Street, Toronto (ON), Canada M3H 5T8
Gazelle Book Services, White Cross Mills
High Town, Lancaster LA1 4XS U.K.

First edition.
Printed in Canada.

Legal Deposit – First Quarter
Library of Congress Catalog Card Number: 2017955482
Library and Archives Canada Cataloguing in Publication
Baeck, Ned, author
Wait / Ned Baeck. -- First edition.

(First poets series ; 18)
Poems.
ISBN 978-1-77183-280-9 (softcover)

I. Title. II. Series: First poets series (Toronto, Ont.) ; 18

PS8603.A33457W35 20118   C811'.6   C2017-906409-6

Contents

Someday, empty handed
I wish to leave this world behind.

Wait a moment!
—Nanao Sakaki

Alice Lake

We adjusted our bodies
to a being
hurt by rocks and lit by stars.
Sorrow no longer enough.
Cherishing shipped beyond wars.

As the old man says: left foot, right foot.
Not a crystal of riveted space
or the backward mercy of being lost,
though strange in our ways
we try till we're crossed.

Driftwood, partially submerged
boulders shone that night. The cold
beach where our warm and promised
forms cleaved, ushering the night
down, and away, and in.

Not the House

A man with pamphlets by the fountain.
Picnics and vagrants in the sunny park
and the women know
what they are offering today,
like a gangplank,
touch with heart pounding.
Hubris falls to the waves.

You can't just walk in here
except when you're young.

You have to learn the stakes
again, handle the precious coin
with respect,
neither defer nor barge in
or you'll end up on the ground.

Some of us slept in the gazebo
up at the mountain,
cold and wet, and the dreadful waiting
when the drugs were gone
and the rainy, dreadful waiting till dawn.

The punks and their dogs
slept underneath the floor
where it was dry.
When the sun was out

I'd sit by a tree drinking beer.
A Rastafarian tossed me a dime-bag
and said, You drinking again?
Don't lose your mind on the mountain
but if you do you can always find it again.

You can jump in the lake
and sneak through that way.
Not the house but the lake.

Calgary Stampede

I hitched a lift east from Golden
with a tough guy in a full-length grey pickup
and unmarked blue ball cap. The conversation
got around to Nanaimo, where I'd recently been,
and the Hell's Angels there
whose influence he credited
with order and prosperity, all the while dropping
the Hell from their name. The trip went quickly,
it's not a long trip.

I had a plan of getting in touch with a relative
I had in Calgary, to see if I could start something over
there.

I was let off at a gas station,
made the habitual collect call
and convinced someone to wire money.
I dread these phone calls,
they are dishonest, guilt-ridden.
Only forgotten by the drinking
they facilitate.

That sorted out, I went directly
to the nearest beer and wine,
was pleased to find
that liquor is cheap in Alberta.
I had cash to last a couple days

and found a secluded spot on a hill
leading down to a ravine
from the side of the parade road.
Settled in for the phenomena
with enough space and dignity
to keep me going for a while.

I remember the grasses, straggly trees, good weather.
I enjoyed the slope and the sounds
of goings-on from street-level
drifting down to my camp.

There's nothing quite like those isolated drinking spots.
I've known many: car parks, beaches, forests, alleys,
or hidden under people's verandahs or in their tool sheds, even
in the middle of a Halifax winter.
Once I downed 60 ounces of Scotch mixed with lamp fuel
in a cabin I set on fire, and tried to fall asleep.

Sometimes it's better than being in a place you pay for,
the drunk giving a fluidity and stateliness to the mind,
a great sense of place as long as it lasts.
And of course sometimes it's pure unadulterated hell
or botched suicide.

But now I was at the Calgary stampede, or near it, anyway.
For two days and nights overlooking the ravine,
festivities carrying on above
and money slowly running out.

When it was time to move on
I looked up my relative, the son of the second
adoptive father of my adoptive father.

It'd been more than ten years, and he was happy to
                    hear from me,
I gave him the intersection
and he drove over to pick me up right away.

Getting in the car I apologized
for a stench I didn't smell but was sure of
and he said, No problem, it's like that
when you're travelling,
but asked me to bathe on arriving at his house
before meeting the family.

The visit began well enough, he and his wife
astute and welcoming, made a fine dinner
with red wine, said I could stay as long as I wanted.
I said my family was lousy and lied about serious things
which in turn made them worse.

I slept on a camping mat in the living room,
remembering as I fell asleep the forty in my backpack
which I nipped at in the bathroom after breakfast
during the next morning's shower,
then again only half-concealed in the backyard.
I had already decided to leave.

Truth is I never make it anywhere
but Vancouver.
It seems to be the only place
I work my nightmares clean.

So after the beer and the shower and the backyard,
I said I thought I'd go back.

He drove me to the highway
going just so far, he said,
to work for both of us.
No hard feelings but some hard accurate
words. Better the evil you know, he said
(His eyes went in to something broken or unrealized—
he played guitar but didn't sing because of back trouble,
couldn't draw enough air, yet his wife loved him,
and his beautiful daughter too).

There was a sign on a bus shelter bench
as we drove out of town: It read
ABOMINATION, there are signs
like that in Calgary.

Hitchhiking back was bad,
not in terms of getting rides
but in terms of who was offering them:
really off-kilter, dangerous people
I had to fend off, mentally at least,
which almost stopped me from hitchhiking later,
at least in western Canada.

I don't remember getting back to Vancouver
or what I did then or if any of it was decent
at that time or any time soon after.

And there were other, longer, more unpleasant trips,
lots of them, though strangely the worst, and also
the worst things I've done, that have disfigured me,
have been done sober. Somehow it is only these
that sink under my skin and find shelter in some
entropic vein.

How Do We Part?

Moonlight. We have a nighttime ritual
of walking in parks
in the wet cold of Vancouver winter.
Our breath rising, our words
sinking heavily down.

Each day we awake
to separated lives. To stay
and to go are each dealt a card.
But how do we part? From our dreams,
our loves or ourselves?
What is the double-bind, besides
divided mind and broken heart?

We carry the gift on our own,

taken
into the throne—
the receding wick
of the candle
burning in the birth,
the candle-changer.

Love and moonlight. The cold has a face.
The healer from here has a body
some crush with their reach.

Who will find solvency, who? Something happens to
dust in the margins, from old peeling thoughts.

Time speeds and eddies, slackens and disappears:
dispassionate and unreadable,
and leaves what? A compass, a hammer,
no fate.

Report from the Ether

The door was everywhere,
and in everything, I stepped through it
back to the house alone.
Sunlight gleamed
off frosted ground, and breath
rose in clouds from my face.

May the world and its authority
collapse in these words.

At that time, going
from street to shelter
to place of my own,
I rented a bachelor apartment
from a Hindu man on 49th
between Main and Fraser—

the nearest intersecting side-street
cornered by a baby blue Kingdom Hall
and a pastel pink Universal Buddhist Temple,
a big Guanyin out front.

I had work with a guy who made
the round of homeless shelters
looking for able-bodied
socio-economic types like me,
it was out by Iona Beach
where the city flushes
its sewage into the ocean.

It was bagging firewood—two of us—
while he split it with a machine saw.
There was a steady breeze
and it stank.

I drank loads of water
and outworked the other guy
and besides his suspicion and the smell
the only disturbance
for those few days
was a crow eating my lunch.

But I lost my footing, paid and hit
the liquor store. After drinking through
the whole of the following day
I sat in the evening cross-legged on my bed,
ready to conceive
of things exactly as they seemed.

The room was next-level,
with a fine stainless steel sink and a pleasing
overall narrowness. My stomach and the crown
of my head tingled.

It was a good solitude,
my heart ticking like heat in a trash-heap,
interlocking histories cutting
easy through my life.

Tinctures and seeds scattered around
the unknown by the familiar.

Silence.
The last job solved
and fitted over mine
clear, clean pain.

I had a magazine
with pictures of paintings of
a man—flesh and blood and clothed
up to the neck,
his head just an outline
framing forest, backyard with clothesline,
highways: unblinking faces that take anyone in.

And on the neighbouring page
the lines, You who are going in circles,
please stop.

I leaned out the window and smoked, carved
one of my own into the wooden sill with a kitchen knife
and drank till my wits began oozing,
daubed and numb
I walked out to get a taxi.

Liz, milk-white Irish
with long black hair, bright green eyes,
ruthless words
and many appointments,
once or twice invited me to her window
so she could bathe my buzzard life in moonlight
and open my heart to its luminous cures.

The taxi waited while I found out, after much ringing
of the doorbell and calling up to her second-floor window,
that she wasn't home, or was but not alone, which is the
            last part
I remember till waking up in my dark narrow room
to the radio emitting the sound of waves
breaking. And amidst this the broadcaster saying evenly,
The waves of Corsica, like a report from the ether.

I turned off the radio, went back to sleep
and by the next afternoon was hitchhiking
to Kamloops: money gone, apartment, job
and belongings abandoned,
pretty sure I still had it
though I might mess up anywhere
I got to—

Sparrow

The greatest ten things
on a plate,

impasse of the hand
order and entropy: between
    they call humane.

I last caved on West One
eavesdropping on my own pulse
until they abbreviated
heart and brain,
overdone
and discharged,

but later made the descent to be
more crooked.

They are here and
call it home,
                burrowing

anxiously below
the sudden, dexterous light—

to attack and drag off the defeated
and run in fear from those who don't fall
into the wet shadows where dementia purrs.

This IS war, and once it has begun
(if it ever did) it cannot end.

The greatest ten things
herded by peons and fates.

The greatest ten things
hidden among dying animals
in dimly-lit crates.

I only look after
my own house now,
when a sparrow falls the land is full.

Reposed in Flight

Basement bright with skin
shows dark, rapt faces.
They hold him
in their hearts and brains.
Someone whispered the world
is not worth becoming evil for—

On the ceiling, which is the maiden mother's floor,
they pound, and pause, and pound again.
Blood pulsing in their fists,
the pierce of loathing under their ribs.

In a shadowed mezzanine
below the conscious mind,
they gnaw on river fish,
direct you to the wrong people,
put glitter in their eyes,
control the atmosphere,
arrange stillborn thoughts in old places.

Later they will say you brought down
the old, dull, rusted sword
with your own hands—and you did—
on the samovar that hid her hand
and the bed where she bared herself.

Motionless,
bird reposed in flight, love for whose sake
everything, murderous and merciful, is done—

It's so quiet now,
vouchsafed to a world of sullen depravity,
a few crumbs of dust for the broom.

The true operation of your mind—follow it—

Intervene

I jumped from a bridge
into the Niagara River
on a bright February afternoon.

It was cold as hell, and the crows
were frenzied when the man
with the hair-lip briefed me on murder. I followed
a dark horse, aware of breathing, maybe not,

there was in falling an ascendant peace
too heavy for space.
Don't look over your shoulder—
unwavering as I hurtle from the rail.

Plunged in and shot to the surface
gasping, voices calling me from shore.
Man woman dog. Saw them as I fell.
Claw cold water till I lose consciousness.

A torrent of electrodes
tears a ragged scream
from my throat.
Nothing has names
yet.

People cover me like insects.
I was in the river.

Maybe I will draw the crocus
and vole of spring
emerging from the teeth of the earth.
Word of mouth

for a warm breeze and a choked song:
watching, waiting,
adjusting to the light,

and when the sun sinks from the sky
I give my anxiety to the night,
settle in to undulation,

the stills and tosses
in the water
lit by the moon.
A forecast
for tomorrow:
the law of today, the lack

a voluminous glint
on our troubled path
by the highway.

The idyll
is a wrecking yard
and the hospital
can't hold you.

Nor mother nature,
though she is
softly pursued,
as we carry out in waking
some of what we have in dreams.

A luminous inner body
through which bitter nettles seep,
poised to enter
the sun-ruled world
and fall apart without end.

From the Bottom of a Wave

Here I am in the abstract-
expression of my precursor's
subaqueous nose-bleed,
the unfurled, dispersing red minus his face.

I hug to the surface, blameless and neutralized,
the cold wet head of Janus.
Dead or alive, his old brain's a weapon,
not a thaumatrope at rest.

It is the lot of the unhurried
that they should proceed,
overtaken by those
who love to arrive.

So, which one?
As apprehension deepens,
sight relaxes into vision.

Conflict is recorded for progression,
not of musical data or phantasmagoria,
almost shocking calm.

We speak, we speak sometimes
together at intervals
of wave-lengths
that may be short but seem quite long.

Impossible to inhabit, turned, shoulders hunched, hands
crammed in pockets, to cautiously unfold
the banal and drastic world.
One is always dodging dice or set upon by rats.

In a procession of objects and indifference and laughter,
various powers babble. One turns
inside out, trapped and burning:
exempt or rejected.

A methodical wind.
A little warm rain.

Protean Things

Maybe to forestall
I go out, though it's already late
and the dark a wilderness.

Armed and drunk,
a fire burning on each shoulder.

Orange, blue and yellow vines
lick the sides of the head,
ears mold to the hissing
pressure of heat, pulse beats out
its duty to blood.

Bones and notes decompose
like eyes, marrow and frequency like vision,
robust and undying.

Flesh will be
laid to waste,
care will be
present.

All our actions tipping
into the grave before and after
us, chastening our claims, here and there
a face, an eddy in the stream, an important address
blending back to unreadable flow,
its brusque gait like a thief's.

Either you want it to last
or you want it to end
or you know it doesn't matter.

There isn't much time.
I'm not saying it's a rush
but there isn't much time.

Already we may have died,
talking decomposition,
although there may be
some kind of composure.
At least the dogsbody, empathy.

There is this limit
and the old growth within it:
degrees and features
at some level neutral, as people
say of weather.

But we die, stop arguing,
stop balancing,
we die
without consummating a wanted
or repulsive thing.

Until then we live it—the cavalcade
and neglected berths at the road-side,
shared with scarred and programmed
animals and images.
Many hard-won wounds
watched over by bacchanals and Samaritans.

Allotted to sniff out
and shrug off the panic,
eyes to rove for stragglers,
stammers of midday
in the ripening silence
so far behind
but still brought to attention
by the clarion call
of protean things.

So why do we think we can separate
our intent from the future, or metabolize
its gruel of almost and elsewhere?

We recoil from the given
as if it were the acid-burned face
of Pangaea, lissome
grandmother, ordinary girl
we have wanted, warred with,
and may even love.

East Vancouver Midnight

At the corner of
Knight and 41st, at the
west-bound bus stop,
outside the donut shop
the rain is falling,
illuminated in an aureole
around the street light.

I don't need to affirm
or negate it,
it's followed by and interspersed
with words.

Some energetic hatch in,
and something going through
is not me, though you might call it that.

The bus arriving that I will board
and the one across the street going the other way
are closer, the rain in the street light
falling alone.

Admit,
you are closer to that
than yourself.

Legal Letterhead

It is night and it is raining.
It was a moment ago and it is now.
There is nothing strange in that,
still, where does the past go?
I don't know, she said, but my body is a house.

In it you may harmonize
like a raindrop in a lake,
a ripple through the moon's face.

And because you are frightened
by relief, made to weep,
broken in—

I'll tell you, this is the way to the heart
of lost hands,
withheld answers,
the anonymity of the dark ones
pursuing you, knowing
just how you see.

The circuit of lullaby
on your mother's lips—
nothing but breath in and out
for 30 years.
The dog-eared page empty of words
for her voice to go quiet
and the child's eyes to grow up against night.

In another sleep
the body turns, he dreams that amid ferns
in a cool forest he is waking up on the ground early in the day.
There is a woman, an old friend, lying at his side, nude and
        awake,
half her body draped over his. She has long yellow hair and
        bright
blue eyes which he looks into, a calm between that contains
heaven and hell, the calm of all their days.

There is a dampness on her thigh
against his hip where it rests
and between her breasts
against his upper arm.

He senses rain is coming, not just rain but lightning.
Nearby birds sing and shriek,
lacerate the hushed, electric air.
Wind brushes his face. Then

he wakes up alone in a room with a dusty fan
blowing air in his face.
He is violently hung over, the room a mess,
he's supposed to be somewhere else,
senses that some kind of line
has been crossed, he's late for work again,
has finally broken off with friends he needed,
has nothing in sight.

It seems everything leading up to this divide
is sealed off, impregnable.
The dark premonitions that dogged his former life
now surround him.

The remains are bare and drained of magic.
He's locked out of himself.

He gets up, sees that he is dressed from the night before,
walks through the open door and down the stair,
where he finds a slip of paper on legal letterhead.

He picks it up and reads that he has been
evicted.

Turnstile

Ravaging enough
that the impassivity
boring through the bottom of the sea
and out-riding the reaches of space
blinks its eyes,
the blackest and surest of cats.

Water snarls as it leaves the sink:
a stark, pervading laugh
that makes the light
in which you hear it brittle.

Life groans
in roses, parked cars,
empty streets,
drunks
and sadists.
Grieves, sheds tears of dust, starry tears,
gazes through them amazed.

      Raw sun, limpid moon.
The taste of trail become path,
uxorious rex
in the lustre of dark hair—
black and bright as the sky at night
beyond clouds and electric lights.

Will you walk with me
through the tender rains
of this city, as it lies now,
although torment is slow
I don't want to go.

Landing

You just go straight railing at your tether—
a spirited dog they say. You can't bear
this wreckage forever—at home in undercurrents,
naked and no one cares how you got that way.
To carry out tasks, to exercise myth,
we accept each other as diamonds in the gutter,
washed by the same worn, inscrutable rain,
with detritus. A flow permeated by indirect light
made painfully perfect your beautiful face, like flattened
cans. Gutted ideas still burning like cigarettes
in a frozen wind, offering one to death,
lighting a match, sheltering it with your hand.
Believe that which plants the immolated seed
of eventual freedom deep in your ear, accepts the smoke
and the light—the changeless hope.

I go home,
close the door,
lie down in bed.

Finally, look into natural darkness,
the beginning-less wonder—how and where are you?
If dreaming, is it there, in the slow
hurtling through our bodies,
warm without indulgence—equally cold,
but the right kind of cold, coolness, really,
a little touched—tied to breathing only, and barely that,
in our region of the Milky Way.

I woke to you, wrote to you,
but didn't know if you were dreaming.

Transformed by living
the fully sentenced seed,
made a broken mind
of a restless heart, tore the rose
and planted weed.

Cool White Tulips

You know I'd rather write
what we'd both be pleased to read:
nothing fatuous or cruel
or cowardly or in greed.

Buoyant words, with brass low
and murmuring, partially
engulfed, partially steering.

There in a park before the dark,
even sea—jaywalking return
through warm hushed streets.

Soft speech on verandahs,
taking leave and turning in, a demure
cat or dog in their generous reaches.

And okay, a lone soul washed up
by the retreating tide
of traffic and mind:
a man let go of through space
but by time.

Then finally, when the crows go east
through the sky to their roosts,
and the grass and the trees rest
assured in their roots,
in cool white tulips
I'm waiting.

How It Falls

Late sun on the clavicle
of an angular woman,
left hip now against a window,
torso arched right, hands in the midst
of putting on or taking off
a thin white shirt, light
straining through her eyes.

You walk alone into a phosphorescent night,
wake up curled in the roots of an elm
sometime before dawn, among ruins.
The atmosphere is familiar
and remembered for its upstream current,
its cold and rarefied air.

You end up there
or accept the code
under your breath in a centre of town,
I have no idea what's going on.

It was a dry spring day in both places,
the noiseless sky crossed by birds and planes.

There is room enough,
space on the ground,
tufts of grass and dirt
on bare feet.

Small rodents bolt
along the base of the walls,
rustling the climbers,
a few birds sing.

At some point
what is it,
the gut-sense inclined
by the universe, inscrutable ...

I'm sorry that populists have destroyed
everything, or as much as they could,
but it is not after all a total free-for-all,

lounging around and plotting the sunset,
if that means anything.

The mandate isn't arbitrary, usually
there's something to be avoided in it.

Even if there's no one
melting faces into one derivative,
breathing for the original,
baiting and lying in ambush.
Wielding the force of stillness

for timely acknowledgements:
animal thrashing, beans and rice,
the apocryphal conscience,
wringing hands.

Sirens probe the silence,
news is generated—
the world recycled every day,
churning words through empty space.

You freeze or move
within and beyond the day, the kind of day
the tide brought in: sitting in a chair
when all other projects have failed,
riddled with scaly looks
in a stream of light as heavy as cement.

Your rising and falling
are the ruins, that is how they continue.
In the first and second person
you make turns
around crumbling walls and twisting trees,
to somewhere you'll lie down.

But the mind's rejections
light the sky almost to blindness,
and you don't sleep.

Still

At the centre of the changing world,
someone with a bag of groceries.

Collective Personal

Seen through the lens
of our eclectic dance
of chance and mischance—
a fleeting suggestion or dream
called home.

It draws us onward—
takes up or lets lie
the vigil
of function and form.

That evolution
will carry on by other means
if you harness yourself
to the ignorance of the world
should not comfort but frighten you.

True, I made to stoop
under a slanted lintel
to meet a feral bride
who called me from shadows
long in the hill.

I had something for her too:
dream etiquette. Ideation
soft and bright as midnight skin.

Sand tossed up, running back
and forth on the beach. Suppose it was good
for the lungs. Those dire mouthfuls
thirsting west, toward the setting sun.

It was that exhaustion,
except when near the surf
where sand is firm.

As for the tributary, you knew at once
to go upstream and be hated for it.

Subject to every transverse hallucination
as you drew near the headwaters,
the ahistorical home of the king:

the single fish and its shadow
on the streambed, the light and water scene.

And it is true, as it has been, the love for you.
There is no dwelling place:
we drop the line and are gone.

Deep Sea Radio

Grace and clarity,
ease and precision
in speech, this is you.

But the vacant feeling
when I rummaged like a beggar
in your eyes, hoping for a morsel.

I'm back in my car
and snowflakes are swirling
into the windshield,
it's late and I'm partially mesmerized.

I remember not driving
and then driving drunk, a terrible kind
of drunk—abdication, flooring the pedal
and killing the lights.

Because one must renounce or conquer
and I did neither.

Shrunken and anachronistic
in this old whale's belly of a world,
listening to the deep sea radio.
Tinkering with sound waves
through cetaceous walls.

Each partially sensible song,
each day returned to,
loved, and found wanting.

Getting By

You stop saying so much.
Things speak for you—

they say you have to close your eyes
and not know how deep.

But because the world still calls
strength weakness
and weakness strength,

you should let your imagination
raze near and distant enemies.
And if you fail in this,

you should provide some form
of enrichment,
and if you fail in this...

A Brother's Sketch

I passed the hunched Knut Hamsun sick-man
in the middle of the crosswalk, red hand flashing—

he going south into the Punjabi village
and I going north, home, across
from the graveyard.

Most days, smoking, I see him from my balcony
overlooking the street—if not on the sidewalk—
scanning the ground for cigarette butts, unkempt
in ill-fitting clothes, the same too-large pants
held up by hands in pockets,
grey-blue k-way jacket, colourless sneakers
rain or shine, winter, summer, slush or dust.

I wonder, did he flash
on mortality on morality
(testing victory truce and failure)
a lot and a long
until his mind detached—
undetermined,
undermined,
stopped finishing his dreams
and couldn't flesh it out.

People think the feeling
you'll die is much. It isn't.
It's not a question of dying,
the trouble is entering

an unroofed labyrinth,
the slight one, but not seeing
your way through.

In your mind a sandcastle
based in the imperishable,
no doubt loved,
being slowly, patiently
licked away—
repatriated—and you still in it
not formed again.

And not being able
to go
where you need
to go
with no other worldly concern
is hell, or at least anguished displacement.
Anyone can tell you that,
and the ingredients are still here.

The mixture of disequilibrium
and just a tiny spout of direct reality
is enough to throw a person.
You might think you're capable
of monstrosity and heroism at once
and long for neutrality like an adolescent
for adulthood, maybe he longs like that.

Or maybe he just wants Lethe,
and to sew up the wounds of memory,
walks without stopping.

Once I offered him a cigarette
and he accepted it reluctantly,
disappearing it into his shirt.
But I could tell I was interrupting
a conditioning pattern,
introducing another blip of potential,
a shipment of blood into ghost-hood,
the possibility of it all happening again.
I haven't done it since.

Purple Shadow

We stacked shoulder weight
and shoulder weight and strode
into the breach, machine-cut grass
strewn with leaves from apple trees
and found our fight
extinguished. What was the problem?
White, exploded flowers?

Purple shadow on our clothes,
on the ground.
No one to find fault with,
no enemy, no end.
And that unchallenged horizon
some prefer
to the sadness life is built of
when the bricks are in your hands.

You can be beaten into agreement,
and if not there's an undisclosed sniper on the ridge.

Now who's that whistling down the path
at your fingertips—

footsteps lifting,
light's throat clearing.

Waters

Friends who do not play both sides,
who are not informants or quasi-agents,
do not wet their hands at asphyxiated springs
and do calisthenics in the courtyard.

Those whose half-lit skin vanishes
like a relic in breaking waves,
notes that lead to assassination song,
beneath their ribs the lyric anti-lyric.

Those guys are all rowing, I'm not saying
we're not all rowing
along some fucked river, passing under
tenebrous foot-bridges
where a few people breathe and remember
sliding along iron-coloured water,
reflecting the sky and the shore,
awake as they still are at dawn.

Threshold

If you discuss a life-diamond,
the tongue forks or thickens
with what belonged to the mind.

You vociferate tone-deaf.
Speech infests the air, like colours
of the sun setting in the graveyard.

Before that, daylight bathed the atrocious human
life of earth in grace.

I remain here, I see
that enemies are often more trustworthy than friends.
They have a truer sense of your value,
at heart a deeper respect for your potential,
which it is their job to gauge and test.

Friends will attack you, fly white flags,
bind your wounds to their hearts.
Enemies just slash or hog-tie
and dump the body overboard. They respect
the dignity of the animal.
A true enemy is clean. When he kills
he kills cleanly.

And for the rest—
some go ignored,
some are actively silenced,
some indulged,
some spoken to evenly.

It's a misery, this life
I've created, yet
somehow I'm free.

I partake of rote offerings,
but not the mean ironies,
the sarcastic comeuppance
of human intimacy.

For love I kindled slender flames
that grew to a decent blaze: for the dancers
in ecstasy, mourners in grief, scientists
and sacrificial ghosts, wise men and women
who smell like the sea and the fields and the viaducts,
the suicides before they jump.

Because she didn't appear, or appeared
as someone else, I curled up
in defeat around a section of coals.

The revelers had gone,
but the ones drunk in their hearts
and the hunter-gatherers remained,
shielded to this time and place,
or by some deeper commitment that consumed them.
I heard their wanton tales.
Then they too left, and their stories
swirled in my blood.

For love I would do it again, I would
watch my mind implode and unravel
for the level, fleeting glance
of your perennial eyes.

I came here for you,
wandered through
the flesh and buildings of this world
on causeways beset by amniotic fluid,
raising my voice all wrong.

Saints offered me protection,
but I was angry or distraught and hid among
lawn ornaments, a dwarf
and a faun chained to cement.

I cut my hands and chest
against the diamond fence
that unites our separations.
Though trying to climb it is a well-known
sign of insanity, I did that too,
and have any number of head injuries
to show for it.

I'm going to approach you at work
crying heaven and hell,
my herniated heart
sinking slow and deep
to my abdomen. A lighted door,
the human face
you pass through, psyche.

In Memoriam

-for Emily Strong

She held a conch
to his ear, he heard
night's point of origin—
wherever it is she's gone:

bright sound,
dark form.

A circle in quadrants:
intersecting lines,
vertical and horizontal
axes, no secrecy.

In one instant see
a yellow-centered
indigo crocus in a sidewalk plot,
without shelter in the night,

and be left crouching,
beholding diamonds of rain on the petals
pointing everywhere:
raised up sad, wondering—

Where did you go? and

Are you alone?

Annealed

We are all bent on duplicating
ourselves. If only we would stop.
You ask if I'm okay.
No.
I think that I think I'm not
is the most okay
thing about me. I guess until we've
gone down and risen, punctured
and sewn up the vision, we'll continue
like this.

That said, I hold certain things true
after testing them against myself,
myself against them, in the stubborn heat
of a Vulcan forge (anything loyalist will do)
with Minerva as my witness,
not as muse or mistress, not even at my best.
A lie, but it had to be said.

Consider the graven expression,
how it feels instead
of the phenomenal thing,
the warmth and coolness
of well-placed abandon,
the common wing.

Exhortation

You hang around
like a fleshed ghost,
rooting for a warmth
you can't abide, feeding
on placenta, nesting
in your own
psychological excretions.

May commandment bear fruit,
spirit martial law.
May our shadows
tread the street
like trained and innocent dogs.

May the right hand hold
and settle the left
in this age of dysfunction,
till it ceases to rifle
the source;
demanding license,
calling it freedom,
demanding moon,
calling it sun,
demanding reflection
calling it origin.
Adhering only to man's law
and making a mockery even of that,
which is only an economic corollary—
whosoever has world-power can choose.

And when the time is nigh,
a solid f**k you and get off the boat.
Jump in and swim with those who take
care of things, for a taste
of god's law: magic, pain and perseverance,
sonar and sharks' teeth and the humble sea horse
that no more and no less
underwrite our days, and are further underwritten
by the bondage of freedom
we are here to enjoy.

But we treat the opportunity as nothing
more than a reminder of our weakness. Absurdly
we take offense. From shame we shut out what shines
toward us and from which falls its shadow,
a navigational gift, clearly indicating a corrective course.
We need that corrective reflex like a beautiful weed.
We need a brain in our head and a heart in our chest.

Kill god, we pretend not to think, and there will be no shame.
Disfigure the light source and no one will recognize
what we have staked: untended, disingenuous lives.

So take your Sunday ethics,
idiot prayers, and die
into life.

From this Side

I saw the shadow
of the herd
encroaching on the circle
of your eye

and I knew
you'd been
helping people.

People need presence,
not assurance.
That's all,
not help.

A deep-eyed,
well-complexioned
Indian woman
hits me
like an axe.

Love will protect
its agreements,
the deeper the stronger,
but not for that less fleeting.

Call to Prayer

The lion stayed all night,
its muzzle on my chest.

I could feel the power
like all potential movement
condensed in a single, crouching pore.

I thought at any moment
it would kill me,
so besides a shallow breathing
I didn't move at all.

Above my right shoulder
a young woman with pale skin
glowing cold.

Down and to my left the aged but puissant
record-keeper, leonine.

The young woman
chill and lit from within.

Her warm mouth, her hands.

Contortionists

Drawn, unhurried, by day sounds:
engines, horns, radiator-crick, voices
from the street, scudding dreams
give way to the room
gradually, like the features
of an approaching figure
growing clear. You know where you are
and openness flashes
through the old place again.

You fell asleep
in a burl of grief:
no lost reality, no sacral bed,
no glass of water or casualty of
riotous animals, burnt down to your tongue,
the acid taste of many cigarettes.

Against it I can't say much:
the straits of doubt
inspired and fueled
this. They were and are the rawest form
of curiosity, answered in themselves,
beyond me, for me. Their harsh
light reliable.

Dread of what comes next
to love and illness:
the apparatus repeatedly slammed.
Which apparatus? The one through which you feel
and think, now in white night's reprisal, a separate course

gnawing real day. No aspirant
says his name here, unless he wants the confessional.

Where's your loving cup? Try this.
We are contortionists,
too exhausted to disentangle ourselves
and assume the primary forms,
so overshadowed by dread
we can't intuit our next move.

A root lifts a rock to dark teeming things,
sways out from its base,
things you wouldn't want on your body,
the saving insight into what is brutal—
brutally lost, embers scattered.
Adult children with flashlights in the park:
here we are with our special tastes.

Remember, it is a graveyard,
stuffed with armfuls of summer night.

Eyelashes to cheek, lips, fingers lightly
trace the arc of hips, small breasts
press against your chest.

For what seems like one quiet minute
you hear the beating of wings,
the slow thrumming of a flock
before they are folded in
in a nearby tree, or on the power lines.

The crow. The seagull.
Free agents, kings, scavengers, rivals,
makers of unmusical sounds.

As a general rule I consider bad things
more likely than good. But only relatively.
It's technical pessimism. Strategically,
I'm optimistic, or I wouldn't struggle with you,
biting in the challenge of darkness
where you live, or bother to return
after drawing near the sirens,
as the body hums with unconscious materialism,
a circuitous exhilaration

and wild prejudice
for love and death.
It might not be your fear
or vigour or recalcitrance
in the face of the momentous—
that you ignore or do not choose what counts,
in whose want you fade.

Remember the dark-skinned wild-haired ancient
Indian man on the corner
who was god—and stood there confirming you,
waiting to cross the street
on evolutionary lines, extending long solar fingers
through the day, into twilight,
gathering momentum and intelligence, the smell of incense
across town, clairesomething. And you went and got in.

Not the one who laughed strangely in a crowd
about Van Gogh in the sunflowers.
Disrespecting his pain and for a moment losing track
of your own. Not the one who helped a drunk stand up
in the alley behind the restaurant,
that old, curved, doughy, high-cheek-boned native man,
he was god on his way to Macdonald's for some juice,
just taking a lie-down on the concrete,
he lifted up his hand and you extended yours. They met
and you pulled.

So you've tasted our little inheritance,
now help yourself to a cold breakfast:
ragged teeth at your heels,
loyal dogs of disorder.
Bloodshot, greasy, glassy eyes
inviting your hydraulic system to flip the lid—
because wholeness slid
down a notch,
listing on the horizon, a speck of rot
across which the razor of perception
cuts a path for you to walk.

And here we are, friend. It seems
that we've come in part to talk this
into being. And grow so quiet in our listening
that fate cannot predict our drop.

Hunched over the Kingdom

Unfolding the earth, other planets, moons and stars,

all-pervading spaces.

Star-belts and galaxies,

they poke around the cosmos—

self, purity, bliss, eternity,

including the unreachable,

stopping nowhere.

But I can't shake the feeling

that someone got out of this

for no good reason.

And that he is still out there,

hunched over the kingdom,

saying things and bringing them to life

and that I can't stop him—

only not succumb

to his siren tears.

Seat

Lost my way in rocks, paper, plastic
in the middle of the night—
blind except for their whiteness
in the moonlight, going north in the clouds,
into the anonymous watcher
who actually has a name,
clinging to the only plant in sight
with fingers worn to the bone.
Gnarled around its whitish root,
they slip from the stalk, and I flail backward.

A life of falling, as though being inhaled
to the floor of a prison more repulsive than spare,
inhaled and held there. It is small, it is quite dark.
The same faint light pervades at all hours.

But the falling never stops, I fall from everything,
I can't stop. Although in some sense alive,
I don't really love.

As a motley crowd
presses toward the empty clearing,
entropy professionals urge that we adopt
the new lassitude, the coprophilic sloth,
and build pyramids to it.

Aligned with the movements of luminous refuse
we have expelled to outer space,
charting our epochal meanness
as if it is an element of nature, as if it is beautiful.

Suddenly locked without stores
in the castle of the poorest lord,
staring through the slat he pissed out of as a child—
expected enemy, expected kin,
someone to blind or be kind to.

Each emissary, friend or foe, offers a forgiveness—
some special character you find irresistible to bless,
because you consider it special,
but that will never be our work.

The walls are high and the shadows long.
Drink dust with Hui'neng till sunrise.

Refining

A kindness sometimes put right,
it's in the rain.

Day becomes night—
an ear for the gravel,
the changing
a silverware too precious to use.

I buy groceries from a girl
with love-bites on her neck.
I'm glad she's making her way
with lanky blonde hair
and confidence, the heart's
straightforwardness.

I forget
a jar of peanut butter
and she runs after me,
into the rain,
Hey, is this your Adam's?
At the bus stop

a dark-skinned man
asks me for a cigarette,
smokes a bit.
When I turn back around
he's gone.
I'm glad because of the rain,

in and out of the streetlights,
the panhandler who doesn't want coffee.
Glad to find you again
waiting for me, you, no one,
listening and refining.
I am waiting too.

On the Grounds of John Oliver

The trajectory seen by the human eye.

The passage of a leaf to the ground,
I can't forget that.
We are witness to perfect
proficiency, sure as silence.

One of the city's green estuaries—
stop off at a schoolyard
under a tree,
empty of kids for the summer.

Take a seat to smoke and drink.
The contact of legs and back
against the grass against the tree,
knobby roots like the back of a hand.

Look into the field
for a moment, empty of human life.
It does not spring through burden
and hunger and thirst,
carrying out and enacting things.

It is us,
however we defend our ailments
and pollute our reservoirs.

The reluctance of acknowledging
that there really is no time
for this,
to go into this.

The sun replete
like after love,
closing shadows full.

Environs of Arusha

My eyes did not persuade you,
my words did not cut through or in.

It wasn't time yet, or was too late.
These and other things are left by the graves
of the space-giving eye
instead of flowers.

Thinking
I am too strong.

Thinking
I am too weak.

Pathless feet, buds clipped by distracted hands.
A stem between the teeth,
damp petal on the arm,
stinging ants found their way into a sandal.

Wait until the poachers shift camp,
wait for the she-lion's kill
and the male's limpid roar,
the trolley of elephant and gazelle
making their evening trip to the river.

We are, all of us, on a flat rock
atop an outcropping before dusk.
Well-perched to observe
majesty diversified on the African plain.

When I remember my way
back there, though I can feel the atmosphere,
the light and the people on warm stone,
there is a stain in that light,
an aural bruise to the people,
an aloofness to the warm stone,
a present restraint flowing back.

And even earlier, standing in a doorway
under an ancient lintel,
grimacing for home.

Entry to Joshua Tree

Alone in the desert.
Alone with someone else.
Away from bread lines
or fenestration, bread lines
or unmoving acrimony. Bloodlines.
Remote eyes. With no reverence
nothing can be. Without it
there's nothing but power
without propriety, need without love,
and you can't properly communicate,
or break down the packing boxes
and run on spirit.

You won't suffer without love,
you'll feel in the dust a cautious insurrection, a cooling fire
and its persistent light, enervated and driving the moon
through the daylight sky like a white fingerprint.

Smooth rocks our feet caress
as we climb to god and child.
Someone on the outcropping
needs to suffer the necessary, that's what they say,
and He did. So he did. We all do, sooner or later.
It's in the approach. We return
to the necessary because we suffer
the unneeded too much.
We have to go home for a while.
Go back to smooth, unstoppable stone.

The feeling commons calmly speaks.
Beholds skin in the dark by touch,
eyes closed and set well.
Old woman at the centre of phenomena—
truly embraced for two or three instants in the passage
of literally billions of years, confined then to human time.

Alone in bread lines of altruism,
alone in a sour-smelling auditorium
where saliva was silently drained from the brass
after the concert. Where staff and parents
clapped. Alone in bread lines of the hoped-for,
in a decaying circuit, the first school of interference.
Days of life eclipsed in a cave,
animal violence in the shelter of the womb, waiting
to start telling how the days are passed, whosoever they are.

Still speak of the hidden corners of the earth—
as if it were flat and possibly private—
of its reaches, as if it were a cat stretching
in an otherwise empty apartment.
Speak of presence of mind,
knowing the code-word attrition.
Say upward when what we mean is outward,
yet upward feels right. And say downward
when we mean awful reduction
into an increasingly dark, hot strain
to be alone, holding at one,
finding the passage and walking
slant-eyed toward pinpoint Medusa light.

Rise

Mute centre
of days in themselves.
Numbered days.

If you must
stay out of sight
of the dance,

do not keep
the bitterness
on your tongue.

Not saying.
Not reaching.
At best

to be in the ground,
to rise in sun and shade.
To allay.

84

Notes

Epigraph: excerpted from Nanao Sakaki's '*Perennial Treasures*' in *Let's Eat Stars*, (Blackberry Books, 1997)

Report from the Ether: The line *"You who are going in circles, / please stop"* is excerpted from Thich Naht Hanh's poem "Going in Circles," in *Call Me by My True Names: The Collected Poems of Thich Naht Hanh*, (Parallax Press, 1993).

In Memoriam: Emily died of a heroin overdose. She was kind and beautiful and a fine artist ... reminded many of true purpose ... is loved and missed by many.

Acknowledgements

I wish to thank the editors of the following publications in which poems in this collection, some in slightly different versions, first appeared:

The Continuist: "Sparrow"

Ottawa Arts Review: "East Vancouver Midnight"

Sewer Lid: "Report from the Ether"

untethered: "Turnstile"

Deep Sea Radio: "Prism"

Thanks to the following people who have helped me along the way: Luciano Iacobelli, who introduced me to the reading and writing of poetry, in and out of class, and guided those interests for years. In 1999, he edited and published my chapbook *Water in the Ocean's Basement* on his press *Lyricalmyrical*; Stephanie Bolster, Professor of Poetry at Concordia University, for her brightness and cool head in holding space for a group of young people; Matthew Herschler, who showed me that gentleness and intense inquiry are not strangers.

Thanks to Guernica Editions publishers Connie McParland and Michael Mirolla, who have permitted me the opportunity to offer this work to a wider audience and to Michael in particular, who has been kind and helpful throughout the creation process; to my editor, Elana Wolff, the book's form and many of its recurrent patterns bear the mark of her selections, and hopefully transmit the value of her close reading; Claudio Gaudio, for agreeing to write something about this book and for being a dear if somewhat reclusive presence in my life.

About the Author

Wait is Ned Baeck's first full-length collection of poems. He is also the author of a chapbook with *LyricalMyrical* press. He studied Liberal Arts at Concordia University and Asian Studies at the University of British Columbia. For the past fifteen years he has lived in Vancouver.